FOR THE FOUR CORNERS

BOOKS BY PATRICIA GOEDICKE

Between Oceans   *1968*
For the Four Corners   *1976*

For the Four Corners
Patricia Goedicke

AN ITHACA HOUSE BOOK
ITHACA

6/1984
am. Lit.

Grateful acknowledgement is made to the following publications in which many of these poems first appeared: *The Nation, The West Coast Poetry Review, Poetry Now, Choice, Sumac, The New American Review, Seneca Review, The Back Door, Epoch, Ms., Poetry* ("Love Song: For the Four Corners," "The Core," "Looking Through the Window at the Future"), *The Iowa Review*.

Second printing   1977

Cover by Petra Cabot

ITHACA HOUSE
108 North Plain Street
Ithaca, New York 14850

Ithaca House books are distributed by Serendipity Books Distribution, 1790 Shattuck Avenue, Berkeley, CA 94709.

For Leonard,
My Strength, My Comfort,
My Delight

CONTENTS

III. THE WORLD PRESSING ITSELF UPON US

LOVE SONG: FOR THE FOUR CORNERS

Keeper of the doorknob.
Keeper of the latchstring.
Keeper of the sword within.

Lakes.
Twins.
Together on the mountain
Rider
Root
Peg.
Tongue obscured
Where earth meets sky
Horseman, flower.
Corncob.
Egg.
Joiner.

I. WHERE WE ARE

MY MOTHER'S/MY/DEATH/BIRTHDAY

Now almost everything I ever imagined
Has caught up with me:
The death defying leap that worked,
The desert years that flowered,
Now the shadow has found a bed to lie down in,
I have come back from the cemetery of divorce:
Having sucked strength
From her tears, turned
Her denial into second growth
Now in my 39th year as if it were the 9th month
Heavy with summer, filled
To overflowing by the good man
She always meant me to marry,
I see him standing like an orchard
Over all the dry days of her dying:
Though the ache of her absence is the first bruise
On the blossoming plum she bore
Now even as the world descends
My mother my mold my maker
Is with me to the end:
Now the hand in the glove of the body,
The soul moves freely and well,
Pockets rolling with the stars of the one man
I always meant to love and now can.

WAKING AT NIGHT

Waking up beside you, for no reason
    Silent as water, in the middle of the night

Is it the slow moonrise
    Up through the toes to the stomach,
        The beautiful bell sounds of nothingness?

Floating
    On the thin bed like a ship
        Now dreams disappear,

The moon like a giant lemon
    The town in my mouth like an orange

The cobblestone streets of the bones, the river
    Blood-red in the starshine

The rocky eyebrows,
    The clear dust of the hair

The highways of my arms stretch out
    Across the desert to you

My next door neighbor, my twin village
    Drifting on the lake of night

The pale steeples of the soul
    Subsided now, and quiet
        Bodies like bright leaves cut loose.

MOVING WITH YOU

is like flying
but then everything is like flying
with you: moving
or standing still,

right now
wheeling like a crazy pony
up here on the roof
of your new apartment building

on top of all the people
lumped, laddered below us
you're wearing your clown's suit
you're so deliciously funny
and so moving

you say any horse
worth his humanity
of course knows what it feels like
to be thrown out, dragged after —

entertaining us at a party
when you do the spastic
walk like a cripple,

fake loose leg,
dislocated jerk,
head and face lifted
above it all, it's obvious

[5]

every move Pegasus makes
with you holding the reins
you're flying, we're all flying
so high we don't notice the pain.

IN THE LIVING ROOM

There's an elephant in the kitchen!
Huge friendly bulk,

Four flatiron feet on the floorboards,
Domed back humping the ceiling...

In the living room the piano sways,
Lifts itself up on tiptoe

Out in the hallway the stairs stretch
Almost as far as the stars

The front porch hums like a harp
The chimney breathes a long sigh
Of relief

In the bedroom where it all began
The cellar sinks
Deeper

Lion tamers and ballerinas
And dwarf butter babies flood the whole house

As she takes off her hat to him,
He lifts his to her.

THE FIRST FORTY YEARS LIKE
A PUFFBALL

This morning I'm lying here in bed
Breathing easy.

Plump pincushion with no pins in it
Relaxed, dusty
Puffball sitting on an old bureau

And the years, yes, the years
Of course will stick more pins in me
As they go by

Still there is no taste like the taste of the clouds
Swirling around this mountain,

Bald hilltop stuck all over with pinetrees
But beautiful, I say, over the red earth
Swinging my arms at the sky

And looking down from the heights of my head
Over the lumps of my body remark
As yet there are few damages to assess

And would have been less
If I had brought you this piece of ground,
This green hummock for you to stand on
If I had brought myself to you sooner—

Then what?
The first forty years like a stuck pig,
Like a wounded porcupine bristling

Inside my own fence, my steel cage,
I had to spend climbing

To reach you.

Now, on this summit,
The thick branches of your arms
Sheltering my nakedness like a fur coat

At long last I am able to look out
And down
Like anyone else the world stretches before me

Behind clouds bleeding, mysterious
But still beautiful, and with a degree of calm.

IN THE HOSPITAL

When they came at me with sharp knives
I put perfume under my nose,

When they knocked me out on the operating table
I dreamed I was flying

When they asked me embarrassing questions
I remembered the clouds in the sky,

When they were about to drown me
I floated

On their inquisitive glances I drifted
Like a leaf becalmed in a pool.

When they laid harsh hands on me
I thought of fireworks I had seen with you,

When they told me I was sick and might die
I left them and went away with you to where I live,

When they took off my right breast
I gave it to them.

THE HOOK

Teetering on the lip of the present,
casting about, casting —
sunbather in daisies,
swimmer in white water,
who would abandon the field of light

to write about it?

My life's too sweet to leave;
I'd lie here forever except

back upstream about a mile
once there was a miracle.

Nearer there's you,
your waterlily face,
Eyes rooted in rock pools,
rainbows pouring waterfalls—

Pierced by the hook of now
my life's too sweet to forget

one minute,

great trout or bluefish
shiny with meaning
against the rush of the rapids

let me drag it out.

THE MELTING

You breathing like a brook,
Your sleep flowing away

Fists the air of the earth
Back with a yawn.

Lumped in the hollows of the bear
With shoulders and back that tell
The long yarns of winter,

By the sack of the body dented
Down by the casseroles of the buttocks,
In the round scoops of the knees

Thick pools of scent
Gather on fur and blanket
Till the darkness is all flowers,

Snowfields pocked with stars,
Daisies matted in the ears
Of those great hairy beasts

Whose frozen presence first announced,
Then melted away but left
Their warm impressions on nothingness,

Spooned bowls of summer on ice.

WHERE WE ARE

And what we say,
The sound of it, echoing
Inhabits the hollow house
With the little ghosts of kisses,
What we leave behind us

But where we are no shadows.

The whole whispering world
Fattens on them like a child
Eating invisible honey

But where we are no noise,

Only a high cloud sailing
On the pale hands of our tongues
White as towers, veiled, airy

Up the stairs to the attic passing
Even the immortal bed which may fade
One deaf day may fold its sheets

But not tonight
But not tonight
Moth wing, flying Dutchman

Swallower of moonlight.

WESTERN

Buttoning up the body
Every morning in a rush

Cramped in, tight
Over the beehive duties

Always they are there
Somewhere

Those vast fields of the soul
Drifting

So heavily and slow
Anyone can ride them: you

For instance, your tall profile
Loping along the trail.

High on the mountains the sun
Like a lazy jellyfish swims

From one flank to another,
All of us

In the shadow of birds, problems
Slow wings passing by

The few ranches of friends,
Waterholes where we stop for awhile

And then move on
Following our own silhouettes, stretched
    out

As if there were never anything but this,
Never anything but these open spaces

Our whole lives, spent
As they really appear.

THE BURNING

This conversation is a conflagration.

Clanging like thirteen firebells you talk
Like a rain of metals, like dumbells
Banging like brass in my ears

So, I think I will turn myself into wet wood.

Ah, what a smoke would be there.
I think you would choke
I hope

But no.

"Listen to me," you shout:
"It is because I love you
Most, like a flame, in full bloom —"

I know, I know.

Sending up smoke signals from my past
Once I thought men were woodcarvers.

I thought women should wrap themselves in cotton
And then go suffocate

But you won't have it,
Thank God here you come

Like a five alarm engine around the corner
You light me, you turn me
Into a clear tongue of fire.

RAIN ON THE FOURTH

Married to you for years and I still cry
Whenever I'm saying I love you.

After the all night party drunk,
Ego dissolved, you tell me

Tears streaming down my face
I told you so again and again,

You laughing but not hard,
Holding my face in your hand
As if you were holding an eggshell.

Now I have returned to the shack in the woods
Where I write poems.

Someone has been breathing here
In my absence!

The windows are all steam
And the floors are damp.

There is a great silence, a cave
Only broken by the trickle

Of the little fire I lay.

Then the windows clear
Like love.
But who is it or what
Breathes us when we die?

This is a very busy poem
For a calm person
And today is the Fourth of July.

Sometimes, down in the valley
A distant thud goes off.

Just listen to the fog
Which makes no sound.

I'm drinking nothing but rain these days
Thinking how much I love you

I still pour tears
Even in brilliant sunshine,
Even in snow.

THE CORE

Blackbird, burrowing
Into my deepest core

You fly straight in
Strong as a snake

In your arms
Strange, strange

Everything forgets,
Everything falls away

Even the glow from the street
Finally goes out

In these black veins
All the animals in the world

In slow motion gather,
Jostling each other with their soft sighs

Turtle next to bird,
Dim tiger, lamb,

Kangaroo, mouse, mole
But here there are no questions,

Here everyone is blind
Hunting the seeds of light

[19]

And we among them, dumb
As two coal miners, digging

Underneath everything for the core
Only darkness ignites.

II. DREAMING ABSOLUTE INNOCENCE

CHILD'S PLAY

The playful young man on the beach desires
To crawl into my womb he says

He desires to throw sand in my womb
Moreover he wants to offend me, to implicate

Me in his little drama, he refuses to believe
It has anything to do with himself

Though he admits the symbol, of course, and Freud
And intellectually paints bananas

And boxes and men crouched
In fear   in fear   in fear

Silence. Dust in the nostrils.
In the archaeological museum

What are these chicken bones
And this skeleton curled

With its knees drawn up, its fists clenched
In a jar the color of sand?

Even in the Old Tribes
The opening was small for a man.

DREAMING ABSOLUTE INNOCENCE

Dreaming absolute innocence in my mind
I rise / rise

Inevitably born to the surface,
Huge baldheaded baby with my snout
Ballooning over the wall of the earth,

Chin on the peak of the highest mountain,
One fist on each of the great powers,
Motherland, Fatherland, in between

My people like toy engines,
The fat bubbles of desire
Rising from where I finally sink

Into mufflers of slimed water, the drowned
Coral rooms of hunger.

NO ONE

All week, waiting beyond the time
Slowly we began to haul in

Rope, seaweed,
The yarn of hope.

Between the two of us we began
Building nests, dirigibles

Began to inflate and float.
O the little noses,

Fish nibbling at the window,
Fists full of blondness

Gradually we began to feel them
All afternoon like bread rising.

O Son, O flower
Daughter we'd dandle between us,

O pillow of softness, how we dreamed you'd grow
Tall as a line to lead us

Nowhere, I said

Or always to this day,
This morning like a dead tulip,

This morning like a cake of soap
With a flat heart.

What was that sound, that wind
Tugging at our ears like the ocean?

O face in the mirror,
Smoke ring, smotherer,

After a long night's knowing
That was no child, that was no one

Coming home,
Knocking at the front door

Like a knife in the groin, like stone
Emptiness light as air

Slowly the balloon rises
And drifts along the shore.

WALKING ON WATER

That day we walked out on the water
Dangling our fins above the echoing blue
Distances our feet could not disturb,
Hanging like glass chandeliers in the depths
The familiar striped fish nosed our wake
But there on the floor your letter lay,
The one you dropped yesterday, shimmering
Among the flowering coral, calmly
White, illegibly scrawled
But unmistakably yours, the single leaf
There on the yellow sand
Shining like silk, shifting with the slow current —
So I decided to dive for it, down through the azure
The aqua the navy the green layers of light
To the bottom, my ears beginning to tingle
Even as the clear vistas turned
Quieter and quieter,
As your mislaid words loomed
Larger and larger —
But long before I reached you the wet tissue
Like soggy rice unraveled:
Suspended in the sky blue galleries it hung
Motionless, the white frazzled shreds
A miniature blizzard of thin pieces of flesh
The fish obviously thought, moving among them
Nibbling a word here, a question there
The gaudy parrot, the inquisitive
Decorous silver backed bream
Eating your words, I cried out to you,
                    Eating your words.

[27]

WALKING AND TALKING / AND TALKING

Like stumbling down a long, straight
White bare road into a distance

This conversation is a tongue,
This conversation is a leap
Into the blank pages of the sky.

Far on the horizon he sees a tree
He does not understand.

His briefcase is full of zeroes,
His head is an anthill.

His woman begins to cry.

Why?

He is a monk walking
He is Tolstoy at the railroad station
In the citadel he is Kurtz.

If anyone is to be exterminated it is himself
Seeing there is nothing and no one
Come down out of the sun.

Betsy, Natasha,
Mother of God where are you?

I am a housewife walking
In and out of the TV commercials
At home my name is Anna.

Somewhere, Christ
And Buddha and Joan of Arc
Are sailing, floating on a bright orange boat of air
Opening and opening their mouths

But saying nothing, going nowhere
Aimless, purposeless as the ocean,
That great tongue of the world swinging—

Teeth of cactus. Stone.
Walking and talking
And talking

Beyond the mountains and past the lake
Finally we have drunk bone-dry

Crickets are calling our last questions.

ESCALATOR

Meeting me it was love at first sight:
You named me for my aspirations.

Ascending with me like a serpent's tongue
Into the one heaven of a department store

You called me water flowing uphill
As smooth, as calm

One foot sliding into
The other and that one
into the next and so

On like a caterpillar unfolding
On bird's feet, precise
Liquid

Jeweled belt going up
Yes truly I am a dream machine
Riding me no one speaks

Electric
Noise bubbles and boils

Like the tubes of a Moog Synthesizer
Yards and yards of me coil
From the basement to the mezzanine

Expanding, contracting, in paradise
Like a zipper silently opening

Up again, down again, smooth
In slow motion hunted

As you, lordly, rise
Without moving hand or foot
Past everything you ever wanted.

THE CHAIRS

There are the chairs
Empty but facing one another

(And then there are resolves).

There are the dresses and the suits
Waiting for me in the closet –
Ho chairs!
Ho clothes!
Without me how do you feel?

The sun on the mountain is beautiful
This morning,
Bright bitterroot yellow.

If I weren't so cold I would stand straight up,
My hair and my genitals would fly—

But as soon as I leave behind me
House, chairs, closet

Everything flattens out:

Nothing will hold anything
Except, in the desert

One or two round red hearts
Stuck on the points of a cactus—

Ho hearts!
Ho cactus!

What's to stop me from killing you for water?

THAT WOMAN

Smudgers of moonlight, black
Streaks and streaks and streaks
All night the dogs run
In circles under my eyelids.

Into the cool well of sleep I drown
Beautifully, but coming up for air
Keep seeing her, that woman
Frozen beside the fountain.

O most innocent shape,
Husband swimming beside me, slow
Peaceful beneath the hill

What was it brought her between us?

Fish of my heart, your feathers
Tangle like chains in my hair.
I may not leave, though I taste bitterly
The poisoned waters of the past —

I have given you all my questions.

That woman your former wife is here
The dogs tell me,
And the owl sitting on my shoulder.

SHE SAYS HIS PAIN IS HERS

The husband in his illness groans,
Paces the floor above.

The hairs of her head rise up
Waving like hungry sea-anemones

But she does not dare go near him
Nor will she let him be.

When will he be well?
Or what is love

That sickens when it finds sickness?

Back and forth her soul sways
Swooning on the heels of his.

All night the salt
Tears fall like bright gouts of blood —

She says his pain is hers,
She cannot bear to speak.

Darling, she whispers up to him,
This suffering is murder.

WHEN I'M NOT CRYING

i'm quite well adjusted
to the concept, thank you,
don't tell me i'm not

thinking of it as something
inevitable, happens to everyone
but Mother, how could you —

quite normally,
even permitting myself to imagine
that somehow, out there in all those abstractions

it is impossible you do not exist
somewhere, in a generalized
but also comforting sense

which i, being your daughter,
take quite literally and
wear your clothes and put on your scent

talking to you meanwhile
figuratively, of course,
since it is only a manner of

speaking but
Mother, where are —
you have not,

when i'm out walking
why is it you're not
anywhere within hovering distance,

sometimes when i think of
it's like turning, suddenly
the foot of your child

on an unexpected stone stumbling
into a huge (surprise)
hole in the middle of the road which

when i think of it, is —
Mother, do you hear me? i'm
falling.

WRITING LETTERS

Night;
Post office of the moon.

Sealed in our envelopes we sleep
Writing letters all night long

Strange words
In strange hands
None of us ever spoke.

Tongue stuck to the rooftree,
Mouth like a broken column

What slow as molasses dreams are these
Will not speak except to groan

Until dawn / until dawn

Steams us open,
Oblivion

Spills over the tangled sheets
The invisible ink fades

Its careful hieroglyphics
Unwound

III. THE WORLD PRESSING ITSELF UPON US

LOOKING THROUGH THE
WINDOW AT THE FUTURE

Looking through the window at the future
under the rooftree of the self
in the log cabin, in the pine woods

and disappearing hills
sometimes it seems the heart
should break from sheer happiness

except that we know our lives

keep leaning outwards
like stone towers into the distance

where the future is lying in wait
with sad eyes looking back
like a huge slaughtered mountain.

THE WORLD PRESSING ITSELF
UPON US

Slipping out of the sleeping bag of our love
Only for a little, to try it
In the warm bedroom, in the city

I am astonished, at first
The air is empty, I am naked
None of your arms enfold me

Nevertheless I must walk
Once in awhile by myself,

Delicately / delicately step
Among the immensities remembering—

Canoes in frozen rapids. Vomit.
Upset. The froth of overturn. Gear
Below zero wet. Dripping. That night

Long ago in Alaska
The two lovers, the friends
Huddled together for life—

Puddles of clothes are drifting
Like icebergs across the floor.

But even in broad daylight, despatched
About my ordinary business
It is so strange / without you

Dressed only in my thin skin I shiver
Ragged as the long howl of a wolf

And though I belong to you only
And would remain with you forever

It is for each of us, alone
Out there in all those Arctic deserts
Teeth flying like snow

Always to step carefully, to remember
With or without each other the question
Under the stars the meaning

The world pressing itself upon us
As if we belonged to it, out there
Eternity hovering / like ice.

THE GREAT DEPRESSION

All of our fathers are old but lately

Lately I am beginning to see
More and more of them.

On streetcars, walking across bridges
In threadbare suits on a cold day
Rubbing their hands together like ghosts

Puffs of sadness flicker above the grates,
Over the subways and windows of the basements

One by one they are beginning to come
Like Eskimos, out of the smokeless North

An army of ancient pushcarts
Gathering like smudgepots to warn us

With extreme politeness and all their belongings
How they left their grandfathers behind them in the
    snow

Which melts, my God, in the spring
The corpses poke up like thin sticks,

In wheelchairs, on canes, crutches
Horned hands begging

Which cannot be avoided, which must
Our scrawny and tramp fears cry out

Like beggars gathering in the dust.

THAT WAS THE FRUIT OF MY
ORCHARD

No moon. No night
    Either.
        White as the inside of an onion

Bed after hospital bed stretches
    Endlessly to the sky.

In the shadowless country of loss
    Wafers of silence whirr,
        Knives like hummingbirds flicker,

Silently they insert the needles,
    The scalpel cuts across
        The entire melon gapes open

And they scoop it out with a spoon
    Silently they throw it
        Where?

I, who was not there, tell you
    That was no nightmare.

Now, even though the scar lies
    Hidden under the grass

Sodium pentothal still blooms
    Coldly, everything smells of ether

And everything keeps murmuring

[45]

Loss is an endless column, cry
    Without sound, mute
        Bird that has flown too high,

And that was the fruit of my orchard
    They plucked

That was the field of my body
    They trampled

I, who was not there, tell you
    That was no nightmare.

THROUGH THE LOOKING GLASS

Looking at myself in the mirror I see you
Hundreds of miles away.

They say there is not much time,
Already your eyes are brackish,

Already your body is a claw
Stiffening there, on the edge of the sofa . . .

What is it you want?
Shall I come to you or stay?

On the other side of the world
I feel my face like a stranger.

Almost I hear you but not quite
Mouthing at me through the glass,

Your arm like a lead weight
Sinks through the hole in my heart,

Already the rags are smouldering
In the hall of the draped mirrors,

Birds wheel around our heads
Heavy as vultures, silently

As if I were twin sisters
You stink, I stink
Everyone stinks of dying

Getting up alone at night
The moon has a mean face,

The floor is bitter to bare feet,
Everything beautiful is asleep.

THE SHOOTING DREAM

I am standing to one side
But both of us are up against
The wall.

Mother, your glasses are dazzling.

I put my arms around you
My last sight of you
For I am about to be killed, too.

It is so bleak here, smells
Like sulphur, wind tearing

Even the sky's paved
With asphalt —

You are not blindfolded.

You will know
The doctor with his needle
When he comes.

But first, after a century
Of waiting
On the refuse heaps of hospitals

We return the compliment:
Here's rubble
In the doctor's eye.

Pretty feeble;
Nevertheless, you smile,

Your glasses are dazzling
And we stand up straight —

In front of his white jacketed soldiers
Those Cyclops, peering through their one eye

It is only after a long, indeterminate while
Having shot us through the heart

The captain of the firing squad reels backwards
One step, and then another
Just before we die.

SITTING TOGETHER IN THE LAMPLIGHT

Past forty it begins.
The houses lose their heads

At dusk, in every small town
Sitting together in the lamplight

Shadows begin to take shape

But no, it is not emptiness
Hearing the news of your death...

In layers of black wool
The moon and the stars go out,

Slowly the seeds take root,
The stomach of the night bloats

In the deep waters
On the underside of town

A delicate coral city grows

And I swallow it, gradually
The rooms fill up, your face
Joins all the others

In the tower of my fingers
Battlements and turrets bloom

Pale stony flowers

[51]

In the courtyard of my ears
Everyone's death comes whispering

Till the black border of the moat
Around my body is beautiful

Invisible, in the sun
But open to the still heavens

And filled up to the neck
With footsteps, flashing remarks,

Fragments of old voices, gestures
Waving like smoke in the grass.

THE OUTER BANKS
(June 6, 1968)

With most of the good men gone, the great
Society itself crumbling,
Out of Ohio through the Blue Mountains
On the day of his death I drove down
To the thin edge of the sea.

The shoreline is different this year.
New gouges, ugly inlets, more
Ground given away

As always,
Even in Ohio, everywhere
The roots of the land are dark diggers

But what is the speech of seagulls?

The rhetoric of love is hunger.
Snap, like a shot
The fingers grab, the assassin's shovel
Swallows whole hillsides in the night—

We are the eaters of earth, eaters
Of the substance, ourselves,
The flesh sliding away to the sea
The trees torn up like teeth

By a seagull's naked beak plunged
Into the rhetoric of death
That is the final hunger.

Back up on the beach.

An old woman like a peasant
Bent, in black, shuffles along
Looking for shells? At her age?

Yugoslavia among the rubble. After the war
Only the crones remain,

But even as the gulls rise
With a great lifting of tattered skirts
Hacking and spitting they cry

The rhetoric of love is also hunger
To pick up the pieces, observe
The woman has a brand-new permanent,
There's a gleam
In the beady eye of every old bird.

It is as good, good enough
As any place to be.

My green bubble of a car pops
And snorts in the shifting sand,
Back of me this huge, proud,
Dark looming land.

We do not understand what
Holds us together.
Like children we keep on and on
Looking for something to blame.

In the forests the fingers of the trees
Knead, twist, hold hands

But the fault's built in, underground
Oceans suck at our weak knees,
The dunes erode, like weathered heads
Grow balder everyday—

What is the speech of seagulls?
The rhetoric of love is hunger,
I want more, the rich

Want more, and the poor—
But here, at the edge of the sea, what
Holds us together is less.

We must build more on less.

THE CURE

(For My Mother, Helen Mulvey
    McKenna, 1901-1969)

1.

Before they knew it,
what had been happening
for years,

the claw of cancer hooked
that gentle Irish
tough pebble of a woman,

Born in Boston, "brought up"
by a herd of red-headed
platitude-spouting bully-boys.

Deaf since childhood, tossed
from one set of loud heroes
to the next,

having hung helpless for so long
in the bleak smokehouses of her sorrow
finally she cured herself:

a glacial empress, tiny
in her emerald gown,

muttering silently on the icy flanks
and mountainsides of her suffering

she turned into a great Chinese lady
and went off climbing alone.

2.
And would not let them come near.

Having brought them all up
to the level of her courage, first

the stiff gray husband, that dour
lame frozen lighthouse,
then the withdrawn, sour
secretly writing daughter,

by main force having wooed them
a little way into warmth,

at last, on the royal throne
of the final kingdom of silence

under the crown of her pain she shut
and locked the palace gates.

3.
In the cave of herself curled up
like a small stubborn animal

in the middle of the vast, glittering
formal antechamber she must have sat

waiting?

God knows what
doing or thinking she would not say

when they had to leave her for the night
never asked them to stay.

4.
As soon drag honey
from stone

sound of bees from silence

for all the gardens they ignored
and she cultivated for years.

Eagerly, flushed with tenderness,
having invited them to the party
the golf course, the sunset,
the passionately simple
dramatic discussions of art, politics
over and over have been refused

in death it was her turn.

Too much on her mind to bother
one could say:

certainly she would say
in the glib irony that helped keep
all but the most persistent pilgrims away.

5.

Speak to me, tell me
I kept begging

over and over wheedling
like a commoner for life at her skirts

this / now / your
suffering's too much

for the fire I left that is empty
for the teakettle turned to stone

forgive us, please
the climate of loneliness is cold

but No, she answered, No...

6.

And still foolishly I kept saying

Spirit of zinnias,
spirit of leaves, labyrinths

Though none may accompany another,
hid in the conch of your ear

is the secret machinery of the verses
your speechlessness spun
from my desperate tongue

not for myself, but forever
for love, for touching
for you to remember, to recite

to lull yourself to sleep
over and over and over
the long hospital nights.

7.
But slowly I began to learn
there is no breathing so endless
as that which will not stop.

And when there is failure of speech, finally
whether of poetry or love
the cure for it is silence...

Yet once / yet

the eyes like wildflowers opened
on the brush of the back of a wind

the fragile hand raised itself
to my cheek and stayed

lifted on a smile that sank
lightly onto the air, wordless

but infinitesimally powerful
"as a petal floating on the Grand Canyon"
she used to quote to me

the impact a poem makes
or a life.